Welc

NAOMI STARKEY

Are you a lark or an owl? Somebody who bounces out of bed at the first hint of day or one who wakes gradually and prefers to linger at the other end of the day? In the early days of our marriage, it took a while for my (lark) and my husband's (owl) preferences to coexist peacefully!

In reflecting on 'morning', we think of beginnings, new opportunities, making a fresh start—and, while many people relish tackling new things, for others the word 'new' is inevitably linked with 'the shock of the...'. Of course, some changes and beginnings are much more demanding than others. Becoming a parent is one of the biggest changes that many people undergo, bringing a host of choices and challenges, and in this issue Lindsay Melluish shares her experience of local church outreach to those who have recently entered this stage of life.

In our opening article, Maggi Dawn shares her experiences as a college chaplain in the unique environment of the University of Cambridge. We also have Jason Gardner writing about the work of the Romance Academy in teaching young people how to handle relationships responsibly.

New jobs are always a mixture of excitement and challenge and it is thought-provoking to read Michael Volland's experiences in pioneering a 'fresh expression' of church in Gloucester. On a much bigger canvas, the 'dawn of a new day' can herald hope and the chance of transformation, and I am delighted that Julia Fisher has written for *Quiet Spaces* on the exciting peace initiatives gaining momentum in Israel today.

Naomi Starkey

1

This compilation copyright © BRF 2008
Authors retain copyright in their own work
Illustrations copyright © Ian Mitchell, Ray and Corinne Burrows, 2008

Published by
The Bible Reading Fellowship
15 The Chambers, Vineyard
Abingdon OX14 3FE
United Kingdom
Tel: +44 (0)1865 319700
Email: enquiries@brf.org.uk
Websites: www.brf.org.uk and www.quietspaces.org.uk

ISBN 978 1 84101 540 8
First published 2008
10 9 8 7 6 5 4 3 2 1 0
All rights reserved

Acknowledgments
Scripture quotations taken from The New Revised Standard Version of the Bible, Anglicized Edition, copyright © 1989, 1995 by the Division of Christian Education of the National Council of the Churches of Christ in the USA, used by permission. All rights reserved.

Scripture quotations taken from The Holy Bible, New International Version, copyright © 1973, 1978, 1984 by International Bible Society, are used by permission of Hodder & Stoughton publishers, a division of Hodder Headline Ltd. All rights reserved. 'NIV' is a registered trademark of International Bible Society. UK trademark number 1448790.

Scripture quotations taken from The Holy Bible, Today's New International Version. Copyright © 2004 by International Bible Society. Used by permission of Hodder & Stoughton Publishers, a division of Hodder Headline Ltd. All rights reserved. 'TNIV' is a registered trademark of International Bible Society.

Scripture quotations taken from New International Reader's Version copyright © 1996, 1998 International Bible Society. All rights reserved throughout the world. Used by permission of International Bible Society.

Scripture quotations marked (NLT) are taken from the Holy Bible, New Living Translation, copyright © 1996. Used by permission of Tyndale House Publishers, Inc., Wheaton, Illinois 60189. All rights reserved.

A catalogue record for this book is available from the British Library

Printed by Gutenberg Press, Tarxien, Malta

Quiet Spaces

VOLUME 10

CONTENTS

The meaning of
morning

Maggi Dawn is an Anglican priest, currently serving as Chaplain and Fellow of Robinson College, University of Cambridge, where she writes and teaches theology. She has contributed to BRF's 'Guidelines' Bible reading notes and is also the author of a number of hymns and contemporary worship songs. She has her own much-visited website at http://maggidawn.typepad.com/maggidawn

> ...seems to sharpen the senses for new projects, new knowledge, **new achievements...**

Morning is a recurring theme throughout the Bible. Some Old Testament characters seem to be 'morning' people: for instance, we are often told that Joshua did things very early in the morning, and Ezekiel reports several times that 'in the morning the word of the Lord came to me'. I tend to be more of an owl than a lark, and, given the well-rehearsed caricatures of students' aversion to morning, you might think that would be an advantage for someone working as a college chaplain. What people associate with student lifestyles might be better described by Proverbs 27:14: 'If anyone loudly blesses a neighbour early in the morning, it will be taken as a curse' (TNIV).

Joking apart, the Bible makes use of the idea of morning metaphorically as well as literally, and as a metaphor it gives two different and apt reflections on college ministry. First, morning gives the idea of a beginning. The book of Job speaks in a mystical sense about the beginning of everything, when 'the morning stars sang together and all the heavenly beings shouted for joy' (Job 38:7, NRSV), but I have more in mind the way that morning is used poetically in the creation accounts in Genesis 1: 'There was evening and there was morning...'. Each time this phrase is repeated, it marks the beginning of a new day, a new phase of development.

A life built around the academic year echoes this sense of repeated beginnings. Ever since I was a child, the beginning of the new school year has seemed exciting and optimistic. There were the familiar rituals of preparation, such as a trip to a nearby city to buy new school clothes, and there were familiar smells—of new leather shoes, newly sharpened pencils and crisp, clean notebooks. The sight of all that unspoilt white paper gave a sense of hope and lightness. This was the year you would work a little better, dream a little bigger, play a little bolder, laugh a little lighter.

Years later, as Chaplain and Fellow in a Cambridge college, I find that each September still brings that sense of newness. Despite the sense of autumn creeping into the air and the promise of winter around the corner, September brings a feeling of optimism and anticipation, like a new day dawning. The crisp air seems to sharpen the senses for new projects, new knowledge, new achievements, new friends.

About 170 new faces join our college community every year and, for students arriving in Cambridge for the first time, there is certainly the sense of a new chapter opening up for them. During the first few weeks of the academic year, the place positively buzzes with energy as lectures begin, course work is assigned and every society and sport and interest group vies for new members. It's an experience that varies enormously from one person to another. For some, it seems that the day has started with sun flooding

---

Work a little better, dream a little bigger, play a little bolder, **laugh a little lighter**

---

through the window and they can't wait to run out and meet it, but for others things start more slowly and it can feel more like an overcast morning at first. Many take time to settle in, feeling homesick at the start, and finding it hard to adjust to the new level of work.

┌ ...I like the fact that there is **an order and a pace to the instructions from God**

Body, mind and soul are intricately connected

One new experience for many students is the sheer pace of life in a Cambridge term. We have no half-term or reading week and it's usual for students to hand in two or three pieces of work every week. Students and Fellows alike find that their feet hardly touch the ground for nine weeks at a stretch. Learning to pace life is a theme that seems to feature strongly in the Bible. God's commands to the patriarchs and prophets often specified doing things at the right time of day. Sometimes he instructed them to be sure to finish a job before ending the day: for instance, many commands concerning ritual sacrifices state that the job must be completed within the day and nothing may be left until the morning (see Leviticus 7:15; 22:30; Numbers 9:11).

Equally, there were times when God instructed his people to sleep first and wait until the morning before starting a task. When God told Moses to go to Pharaoh and demand that the slaves be released from Egypt, we read that the Lord said, 'Get up early in the morning and confront Pharaoh' (Exodus 8:20, NIV). 'Why wait till morning?' you might ask. If God has a plan, why not get on and do it right now? It's a reasonable question but I like the fact that there is an order and a pace to the instructions from God. The sense that there is an urgency about obeying God doesn't alter the fact that tasks have a right time. Learning to pace ourselves is important.

For all Cambridge students, there are always multiple activities they could be doing, and learning to choose between them is a life skill that's vital for success and sanity. One of the things I say repeatedly to students, especially during revision for exams, is to keep regular hours: work hard through the day, eat properly, exercise and get some sleep. Of course, there are always exceptions to the rule and there are a few who seem to flourish by burning the midnight oil, but, for most people, a good balance of rest and work, food and exercise, is what produces the best results. Body, mind and soul are intricately connected and for the most part we need to keep life in balance.

The student population is, of course, transient, but another section of the college community is made up of Fellows and support staff who have

long-term posts. What does the idea of morning have to say in the context of permanence and stability? An image that recurs in the Psalms and the prophets is the promise of morning as a metaphor for hope, and this is valuable at times when people are affected by illness, family problems or a death. One of the strangest feelings that accompany times of darkness is the realization that the rest of the world continues to turn as if everything is normal. The sun still comes up in the morning, the buses still come and go, and the bereaved or depressed person wonders at the audacity of the world. Why doesn't everything stand still when your own life has ground so painfully to a complete halt?

A good balance
of rest and work, food and exercise, is what produces the best results...

At times like that, we need friends and ministers who understand the darkness. There's nothing worse than a Job's comforter who tells you that if only you behaved a little differently, everything would get better. Sometimes, as Job knew, you do all you can and the darkness still falls. But the promise of morning is a poetic image that the psalmists throw out

There was evening and there was morning...

into the darkness as a thread of hope: as surely as day follows night, light will come in the darkness and joy will follow pain. 'Weeping may linger for the night, but joy comes with the morning,' writes the psalmist, stubbornly hopeful in the face of despair (Psalm 30:5, NRSV).

This image can be equally important to students. It's easy to assume that young people in a creative and independent phase in their lives are endlessly happy and carefree, but many students—and young academics as well—struggle intensely with stress, anxiety and depression. The reasons for this would fill a whole book but, given that it is the case, a significant part of my work is the care of depressed and anxious

people. Alongside various other agencies, chaplaincy ministry is a vital component in supporting people who are struggling.

It's hard to understand, unless you've been there yourself, just how densely black things can look when you are depressed. For some people, days and weeks can go by in unrelieved shadows of bleakness and it is hard to make hope real to someone at such a time. I find it a relief to note that both prophets and Psalms paint a thoroughly realistic picture of life at its darkest.

It's tempting to feel that a minister of the gospel should always offer hope. Sometimes, though, for a depressed person, the acknowledgment that the darkness is indeed very dark offers more hope than words, however sincerely meant, which seem to suggest that you don't understand the depth of hopelessness someone is experiencing. In this kind of desperate situation, the psalmist again uses the image of morning, but this time as the morning that refuses to come: 'My soul waits for the Lord more than watchmen wait for the morning, more than watchmen wait for the morning' (Psalm 130:6, NIV). They say that the darkest hour is just before the dawn, and if you've ever suffered from insomnia, you'll recognize that sentiment.

One of the worst nightmares of any educational institution is the death of a young person. Not often, just every now and then, a life is lost through accident or illness, but perhaps worst of all is the instance when someone loses their battle against despair and ends their own life. Walking alongside a bereaved community is one of the most stretching but perhaps one of the most important tasks a chaplain carries out. When a young person dies, it is often their friends' first experience of the death of someone close to them or of someone their own age. It's a moment when the fragility of life and the sense of one's own mortality suddenly become a stark reality.

Some years ago, I led a memorial service for a student who had, tragically, ended his own life. I remember concluding my address with the words, 'His life has ended, but now our lives have to go on without him.' I choked on tears as I said it, knowing that although he had lost hope, his friends now urgently needed to rediscover it. We sought ways of commemorating his life together over the weeks that followed, reading and talking together, playing his music and planting a tree in the college garden in his memory. Not all the students I was talking with shared my faith but I sought ways to restore to them the sense of 'a future with hope' that Jeremiah spoke of (29:11, NRSV).

A final thought about the meaning of morning in the Bible sums up for me the heart of what college chaplaincy is about. In John 21 we read, 'Early in the morning, Jesus stood on the shore, but the disciples did not realize that it was Jesus' (v. 4, NIV). A great deal of chaplaincy work involves offering welfare and pastoral care to people who do not share my faith and do not perceive God at work in their lives. I have come to see that this is no barrier to the working of God's Spirit. God, it seems, is generous with grace towards people who do not recognize him at all.

To be a Christian chaplain in a community of mixed cultures, faiths and experiences is to be a minister of hope, someone who embodies the belief that 'joy comes in the morning',

Chaplaincy ministry
is a vital component in supporting people

someone who knows how to find calm in a crisis and hope in despair. Some may never find faith, but every now and then an ex-student will return, sometimes years later, to seek me out and tell me that along the way the penny has dropped and they have indeed discovered faith for themselves. When that happens, I am reminded again of morning—both as a new phase of life and as a symbol of hope. 'There was evening and there was morning...'—a new day! ■

Attracting and keeping young families

Lindsay Melluish is married to Mark, who is a vicar, and they have five children. She is on the staff of their church, St Paul's Ealing, and is also part of the leadership of New Wine Conferences, where she is a regular speaker. She and Mark have written 'Family Time', a book and parenting course (Kingsway, 2002) and she has also written one of BRF's 'Bible Readings for Special Times' booklets: 'New Baby'.

Just over a year ago, I was invited to a wedding in our church. It was a wonderful celebration—the coming together of two young people who had met through church. Just last week we visited this same couple in their new home and met their brand new baby, a beautiful baby girl.

Yesterday, as we were reflecting together as a family over the happy events that had taken place recently for them as a couple, my 13-year-old son said, 'Mum, have you noticed how they've started coming to the morning service on a Sunday since they've had their baby?' It was true: since their marriage they had only ever gone to church on a Sunday evening but now, with a new baby, that was evidently going to change.

In a sense there's nothing unusual about that little scenario. It's probably more practical for them to attend a morning service now that they have a small baby. But as I thought of them, I thought of others, too, who have changed their habits of church attendance depending on their family circumstances. One mum who has attended in the mornings with her three children for many years has recently started coming in the evening, where her children, now teenagers, come with their friends and where her own friends—parents of teenagers themselves—also attend. Another family, who never used to go to church at all, have started coming to our morning service (where there are children's groups) because their children have begged them to, so they can see their school friends on a Sunday as well!

As I've pondered on the movements of these and others in our church, it's struck me again how people love to link up with others who are in similar life situations to their own. Most are motivated to look for relationships with like-minded people who are at the same stage in family life, with whom they can share life, whether they are young or old or somewhere in between. That's why people sign up for National Childbirth Trust classes when they're expecting their first baby or join a tennis club when they move to a new area. Some people, when they decide to stop having children, then get a dog and meet other dog owners in the park every morning!

All of this has huge implications when it comes to church ministry, in terms of encouraging and discipling those within the church, and of reaching out to those currently still outside. If your desire is to target parents with young children, to create within your church a healthy community comprised not just of the older generation but of young families too, there will be certain key questions you can ask yourself. The answers will be very helpful in enabling you to fulfil that desire.

When families come to this church, do they get a warm welcome and feel that their children are just as welcome as they are?

A healthy community comprised not just of the older generation but of young families too

A warm welcome is crucial. I love it when I enter a place, be it a party or any social event, large or small, and someone approaches me, smiles and says they're glad I'm there. People love to feel wanted, and if they believe you're glad they're there, they will relax and have a much more enjoyable time. Even better, if they believe you're glad their children are there, they'll have an even better time and will probably want to come back.

Are there other people here to whom young parents can relate and share life together, and are we creating opportunities for families to make friends with one another?

If you're parents of young children yourselves, you're immediately at an advantage and have a readymade

... a desire to use what spare time you have to share your faith with others

opportunity to invest personally and intentionally by befriending and mixing with other families, perhaps by inviting them round for Sunday lunch or Saturday tea, by being willing to share your lives with those you want to draw in.

If you're not at that stage, it's a bit harder but by no means impossible if you're really motivated: you can look for ways of creating an arena for families to link up, maybe by hosting a barbecue or picnic, or running a parenting course on a Sunday afternoon (with childcare) to enable parents to tackle together some of the issues that everyone faces in family life at one time or another.

Will the children have such a good time that they want to come back next week?

It really is true that parents will often do quite surprising things if it means their children are happy. If their children love the church children's groups, the whole family is far more likely to want to return next week. That means making a priority of investing in the children's work. It means giving the children's work the best leaders you have (and plenty of them) rather than just sending the children off with anyone who will take them and hoping for the best. It means putting money into enabling those leaders to attend a children's workers' conference. It means someone, probably the church leader or someone in authority in the church, putting aside time to sow vision into them and encourage them in all they are doing. And it means putting money into buying toys and equipment to enable them to put on a programme that is properly resourced.

Those are challenging questions and they won't be answered overnight, but when they are answered, the resulting work will bear much fruit.

That's Sundays—but Sundays really are just the beginning. There are six other days, often bringing more possibilities than a Sunday for attracting parents and young children, and depending on where you live, there may be nannies and child minders to draw in as well.

Maybe you're a full-time church leader or worker who is longing to draw young families into your church. Maybe you're a parent who is at home full-time with little ones but with a heart for evangelism and a desire to use what spare time you have to share your faith with others. Maybe you're at home for some of the day and would love to use your time in reaching out to those who are also around in the daytime.

There's a world that happens between 9am and 5pm in the local community, which people who work full-time barely know about. A pregnant woman who stopped work to have her baby recently said to me, 'I just didn't realize how much goes on in the daytime. It's a whole new experience!'

In many areas, if not all, there's a network of people around in the daytime, many of whom are looking for activities to give structure to their hours, especially if they have care of children. Early parenthood is often a time when women's hearts, especially, are at their softest and they tend to be more open to finding out about faith. Maybe they were brought up to go to church themselves and like the idea for their children, so they're thinking about coming along.

What an opportunity to invite them to a toddler service at your church with delicious cakes and fresh coffee, interesting toys for their children to play with, and a friendly team of people to host the event! If they come

to that event long enough to feel at home in your church and make friends with others who go there, they might be inclined to accept an invitation to do a daytime Alpha course, especially if there were more delicious cakes and fresh coffee and well-run child care for their (by now) toddler and second baby.

When they've completed their Alpha course, they might even be tempted to bring their husband along for a parenting course or a marriage course, or simply join a daytime small group to study the Bible, support one another in prayer, and of course consume more delicious cakes and fresh coffee…

These are some of the events that run in the church I'm part of, but you've probably been thinking of your own, much better ideas, events that would work well in your context and would gather people together as

---

There's a network of people
around in the daytime

---

community. How exciting to think that you could be instrumental in encouraging that couple who has just had their first baby to get truly linked into your church community, bringing others with them and enabling your church family to be balanced and healthy, a coming together of all ages—which, after all, is just what a family should be. ■

The dawning of peace in the
Middle East

Julia Fisher is a writer and broadcaster with a particular interest in Israel and the Middle East. She is the author of a number of books (details on her website, www.juliafisher.org) and is currently working on another book developing the theme of God's purposes for Israel in relation to the rest of the world.

It has to be said: my book *Israel: the Mystery of Peace* (Authentic Media, 2004) is a collection of rather bizarre stories. The hypothesis of the book is that there is peace in the Holy Land between Jews and Arabs today. 'But,' you say, 'how can this be when tension frequently erupts, people die and hopelessness hangs like a cloud over the region?' I agree with you! However, I have seen this peace with my own eyes and spoken to those concerned, and these true stories are proof that something is quietly happening that not many people currently realize: a peace movement is gaining momentum in Israel today.

I stumbled across these stories almost by accident. In 1997, while working at Premier Radio in London, I had a conversation with a fellow presenter, Olave Snelling. We talked about the need some women have for a short inspiring break—a time to travel somewhere exciting, pray and be taught the Bible. The idea of a tour to Israel was born: 'Women of the Book'. Olave led the first tour in June 1998 and I led the second in the following November.

Being a tour leader was a new and amazing experience—travelling with 50 women from many nationalities. But it was on the plane home that something unexpected occurred. I was very tired, though relieved that we had enjoyed a successful tour. And then it happened. Just as I was dozing off to sleep, it was as though somebody spoke to me: 'Wake up, Julia. Write this down.' In an instant I was fully alert and reached for my notepad. 'In six weeks you will be back in Israel. You have seen the land and visited the sites but I am bringing you back because I want you to tell the stories of what it means to be a believer, whether Jewish or Arab, in Israel today.'

Was I imagining this? There was only one way to find out and that was to wait and see if it happened. I didn't tell anybody about what I had experienced.

The invitation to return to Israel arrived almost immediately. The Israeli Government Tourist Office was inviting journalists to view some new hotels and tourist sites that were being prepared for the millennium. Israel was expecting that during the year 2000 the usual number of tourists would increase from one million to three million, and they wanted to show us that they were ready to welcome the crowds.

The trip was planned for early February 1999 and, despite a packed schedule, I was able to clear a couple of days at either end to start my 'research'. But where should I begin and with whom? I knew

> I was very tired, though relieved that we had enjoyed a successful tour. And then it happened...

One area in particular caught my imagination: **reconciliation**

They share a common faith in their Messiah

nobody in Israel well enough to ask for their help. I didn't even know what the state of the Church was in that country, let alone how many believers lived in the land.

I started to read articles by Christians who worked there and one area in particular caught my imagination: reconciliation. This was before the recent *intifada* had begun but, even so, I was reading some intriguing stories of Jewish/Arab initiatives and Christian/Jewish projects.

As the date for my departure drew closer, I heard on the grapevine that that there was a breakfast meeting for pastors in Jerusalem the morning after I was due to arrive. How could I get to meet these people? All I could do was pray and wait for God to lead me to the person who would open that door. If this sounds as though I was quite nonchalant, let me assure you that I was finding it hard to trust God in this way and at such a late hour. To be honest, I was saying to the Lord, 'Why choose me?'

Then came the first sign of a glimmer of a breakthrough. On the night before I was due to leave, the phone rang. The caller said, 'Julia, there's a man called Ray Lockhart on your plane to Tel Aviv tomorrow. He's the rector at Christchurch in Jerusalem and knows many of the local Christian leaders in Jerusalem. Here's his number; he's staying in London tonight at his daughter's home.'

Early morning in Jerusalem is full of promise. The air is fresh, the light bright...

Poor Ray—to have a call from a radio journalist asking to meet him at Heathrow the next day! He had every reason to say no, but he didn't.

'How will I recognize you?' he asked.

'I have a yellow suitcase,' I replied.

Ray found me at the airport and, as we chatted, he asked me what my 'mission' was. I told him simply what had happened. He could have discounted my story because, let's be honest, there are some crazy 'Christians' around who get a 'thing' about Israel.

Ray listened attentively and then said, 'There's a breakfast for pastors in Jerusalem at 7 o'clock tomorrow morning. They don't usually welcome visitors, especially journalists, but come and be my guest.' We arranged to meet outside Christchurch, by the Jaffa Gate, at 6.30 the following morning.

Early morning in Jerusalem is full of promise. The air is fresh, the light bright. I awoke to hear sparrows chirping loudly outside my hotel window and, being in Arab east Jerusalem, I could hear the call to prayer from a nearby mosque.

Ray opened the meeting. Some had travelled quite a distance to be there. I think I was the only woman present. I could hear a number of languages being spoken, including Hebrew and Arabic. I now realize that these meetings provide a valuable opportunity for the exchange of news between people who normally wouldn't meet.

Ray introduced me to the assembled group: 'Tell them why you're here, Julia.'

It didn't take long. I told them my story and said that I would be available after the meeting if any of them felt they would like to tell me about their work. And so it was that I started to hear what it meant to be a believer in the land of Israel. I met Dr Gershon Nirel, a Messianic Jewish believer and director of *Yad Hashmona*, a Messianic kibbutz-style community between Jerusalem and Tel Aviv. I also met Dr Salim Munayer, an Arab Christian and the founder of the reconciliatory organization, *Musalaha*.

At that meeting, friendships were forged, and over the past ten years I have been back to Israel over 30 times. A few months later, the *intifada* began and the stories I was researching started to take on a whole new meaning. Reconciliation between 'enemies' is, I have observed, only for the brave.

As well as meeting believers involved in reconciliation between Jews and Arabs and Jews and Christians in the Holy Land today, certain verses in

And so it was that I started to hear what it meant to be a **believer in the land of Israel**

... enables them to transcend politics, overcome their prejudice and distrust, and enjoy a peaceful coexistence

the Bible have also influenced my thinking and convinced me that the coming together of Jewish and Gentile believers at this time in history is no accident but is actually part of God's plan. For example, the letter Paul wrote to the Ephesians mentions 'God's secret plan' to reconcile Jew and Gentile, and speaks of how 'God's purpose was to show his wisdom in all its rich variety to all the rulers and authorities in the heavenly realms. They will see this when Jews and Gentiles are joined together in his church' (Ephesians 3:10, NLT).

Was I witnessing something in Israel today that had not happened since the early Church started 2000 years ago? This realization started to dawn on me and the stories in *Israel: the Mystery of Peace* began to emerge. Yes, the number of believers in the Holy Land is relatively small. Yes, the people are challenged to their core: for both Jewish believers and Arab Christians, pressure from their own communities, let alone from outside, is sometimes overwhelming. Yet reconciliation is happening.

Something is quietly occurring in the Holy Land today that has nothing to do with politics but everything to do with the Holy Spirit. Gentile Christians are involved as catalysts between Jews and Arabs; Jewish and Arab believers in Jesus realize that they share a common faith in their Messiah, which enables them to transcend politics, overcome their prejudice and distrust, and enjoy a peaceful coexistence.

They believe that Jesus is returning to his Church—a Jewish/Gentile Church. This is not a popular view—many Christians would vehemently disagree with it—but for those involved in this movement, it is their understanding of what the Bible says. It would also appear, from the evidence to date, that the peace being forged is genuine and is withstanding the heat and pressure from the political climate round about.

I wrote *Israel: the Mystery of Peace* to introduce some of these people to the Church in the West. None of them is famous. They don't have big, powerful organizations behind them. But what they are doing—or, to be more correct, what God is quietly doing through them—deserves to be told.

I visited Israel, the West Bank and Gaza during 2002 at a time when trouble and tension were ever-present. Suicide bombings and other acts of terrorism were happening daily. Many people were dying. Tourism had declined to an all-time low. The country was gripped by a sense of despair: all hopes of a peaceful settlement between the Israeli government and the Palestinian Authority had been dashed. Many attempts at reconciliation and peace-making had failed, especially in the political arena, yet the work of the believers was flourishing. I was seeing something good emerging from the chaos. I was witnessing, at first hand, reconciliation, unity and cooperation between Jew and Arab.

Maybe the world is about to see God do something in the Middle East that will surprise even the most sceptical. Once again, the Jewish people are being vilified by certain political and religious ideologies that want them eradicated from the face of the earth. At the same time, Palestinians are widely seen as being Islamic fundamentalists: the minority Christian voice within this Arab community is barely heard. All the average Israeli man on the street wants is peace; likewise his Arab neighbour, but it seems to elude them both. Nevertheless, it would appear that we are starting to see God's 'mysterious' plan dawning. ∎

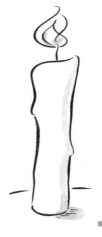

A peace movement is gaining momentum in Israel

Reconciliation between 'enemies' is only for the brave

Pioneering *growth*

Michael Volland spent six years as a youth worker before training for ministry in the Church of England. He has also written 'God on the Beach' (Survivor, 2005) and 'Going to College' in BRF's 'Bible Readings for Special Times' series.

On a Sunday morning in July 2006 I was ordained deacon at Gloucester Cathedral. I knelt with my fellow ordinands, waiting for the bishop to lay his hands on my head and call on the Holy Spirit to equip me for the office and work of a deacon. I listened as others around me were ordained to this or that parish. As my turn came, it was not the name of a parish that the bishop announced, but a new role: pioneer minister in Gloucester city centre.

I was one of a handful of ordinands to make history when the Church of England ordained the first batch of pioneer ministers—or, to put it in layman's terms, ministers with a broad brief to 'reimagine' and grow church with those who are nowhere near the church.

My commission was to plant a Fresh Expression of church in Gloucester city centre with those aged roughly 18–35 (the demographic most obviously absent from the national church in the UK). I was given no building, no plant team, no major financial resources. As I made a start, I would be drawing on my past experience, my training at theological college, my wits and, more importantly, the guidance of the Holy Spirit.

I was excited. I didn't have a clue whom I would meet, what we would do or where we would do it. It would be an adventure and I would look forward to seeing what emerged.

It's worth mentioning that one of the ways in which my situation is 'peculiar' is that alongside having a brief to grow church in the emerging culture, as a curate I am rooted in the worshipping community of Gloucester Cathedral. My incumbent is the canon missioner—part of the cathedral's chapter; I have a rhythm of daily prayer based in the cathedral, I attend the Sunday eucharist and am heavily involved in services at festival periods such as Easter or Christmas.

It is almost as if I have one leg in the institutional church writ large, and the other in a culture that couldn't seem more distant. Since making a start, I have found that being based at the cathedral has given me not only a home in a praying community but also an invaluable working insight into an ancient tradition of church that is outside my previous experience. The richness of this tradition and its potential for re-presentation to those outside the church is becoming more apparent to me as time passes.

I am writing this ten months after being ordained, and it certainly has been an adventure. Through a mixture of prayer, relationship building and creative thinking, a dynamic community has begun to emerge and there are many stories to tell.

Perhaps the one most suited to telling here is from the very early days of the project, before anything had begun to grow. I suppose it is a story of the first acorns being pressed into fertile soil.

After my ordination I began to pray and to meet people in the city. I found church leaders galore (there are 75

A picture of the city's spiritual life began to form...

... a story of the first acorns being pressed into fertile soil

churches in the city), youth workers, chaplains, laypeople, evangelists, college lecturers, school teachers, musicians, artists, journalists, bar staff and lots of others who didn't fit into any particular category.

As my first summer in Gloucester unfolded and a picture of the city's spiritual life began to form in my mind, I found myself regularly praying a prayer that went something like this: 'Lord, you've brought me to Gloucester, and that's great, but if you've got growth in mind, then you'll need to send someone my way to help kick things off. Sooner would be better than later, but whenever's good

for you is fine with me too… Amen.'

This was the prayer on my lips one Monday morning in early September. I had been walking in the city's docks area and was sitting beside a large, crumbling sailing ship. As I looked at the ship, I asked God to send me someone to work with. After five minutes or so, I got up and walked towards home.

I could see from some way off that the front door of my house was open and, as there was no sign of my wife or children, I wondered what might be going on. Upon reaching the house, I stepped tentatively into the hall and peered into my study.

A tall, well-built young man with a shaved head was stooping over my desk, scribbling something on a pad. My wife was also in the room, holding my diary. I raised an eyebrow and cracked a welcoming smile, and all at once they both began to explain that this was Dan, who had come to find out if I was starting a church and was leaving his number so that I could get in touch.

I beamed at him and asked if he had a minute to talk. Two hours later, we were still going. Dan explained that he and Ruth, his wife, had grown up in Christian families and studied theology as undergraduates but that, as life went on, they had found it increasingly hard to feel settled in church. The world that many of their non-Christian friends inhabited and the world of church seemed so far apart, and there appeared to be little chance of any of the friends making

the cultural leap into church without serious damage.

As Dan explained this, I realized that he could be telling my own story. I had worked through exactly the same experience.

At the heart of the gospel was a person that Dan and I loved, and a message that we wanted to live, but so much in today's church life seemed unwittingly to have wrapped the gospel up in cultural clothing that was less and less relevant. The problem was that the gospel and the cultural baggage had become confused for

We are an emerging worshipping community

many Christians and, instead of recognizing outmoded ways of worshipping and of structuring church life generally, churches simply continued to hope and pray that new people would come through the doors and find Jesus.

This wasn't just ancient parish churches clinging to the Book of Common Prayer, either; this was every denomination, including the 'free' churches, many of whom were stuck singing popular choruses from the 1980s and still operating their outreach entirely on a 'come to us' basis.

Dan and his wife had spent a year in Australia with a network-church that met in cafés. They had found it powerful, relevant and full of Jesus. They had come back to the UK wondering whether to start something similar in Gloucester, and had spent the preceding nine months praying and hoping.

We are rooted in Jesus Christ and are seeking to serve and follow him

On the Friday before we met, Dan had had enough. He'd told God exactly how he felt. 'We need to meet with others who feel like us soon, Lord,' he prayed, 'or we're going to go crazy.' The next day he called in at an old friend's house. The friend asked him about church and began to make suggestions about where he might try. At the bottom of the list, and when Dan was preparing to leave, my name came up. The old friend happened to be someone I'd met and spoken to about my work the week before.

Dan's ears pricked up. It was a long shot but he wondered if this could possibly be what he and Ruth had been praying for. Sunday passed, and first thing on Monday morning Dan decided to find my house, knock on the door and ask me if I was up for 'doing church' in new ways to reach the people furthest from traditional church.

I still find it amazing that while Dan was searching for my house that morning, I was sitting at the docks praying that God would send someone along for me to work with.

Dan and Ruth came for dinner with me and my wife shortly after this first, peculiar meeting. We decided to get together each week for a meal and some worship. Soon someone else joined us, and then another person, and after this a young couple and, as the months passed, other people got involved in events, parties, meals, being at the pub, discussing faith and generally living life together.

We are an emerging worshipping community, part of the global and historic Church and committed to sharing our lives with each other. Our corporate life is organic and exciting and genuine. Most important of all, we are rooted in Jesus Christ and are seeking to serve and follow him in the 21st century. This is the early morning of an expression of church fit for living the gospel in our generation, and it's worth saying that at the time of writing there has been no transfer growth from any local churches. Please pray for us! And if you're ever in Gloucester, look for us (or visit www.feig.org.uk). ■

At the morning of our lives

Martyn Payne is a member of BRF's Barnabas Ministry team, working in schools and churches with teachers, children's leaders and children. He has also worked as the National Children's Work Coordinator for the Church Mission Society and taught in London schools for 18 years.

How clear and fresh is the sound of birds singing in the early morning! It's that moment of the day when creation can be at its most audible. It is also a good time, according to the psalmist, for conversations with God—a time to hear and be heard by the God of creation.

This possibility of 'revelations at dawn' seems also to apply at the dawn of our earthly life. Young children can often hear the voice of God more clearly than we who are burdened by the busyness and noise of the day.

> 'Lord, in the morning you hear my voice. In the morning I pray to you.'
> PSALM 5:3

Indeed, Jesus says as much when he gives thanks to his Father that the mysteries of the kingdom are 'hidden from the wise and understanding but revealed to his little ones' (see Matthew 11:25). Ask anyone who

... the remarkable insights into spiritual truths that children can bring

works regularly with children and they will tell you of the remarkable insights into spiritual truths that children can bring. Many of our reports from *Barnabas* RE days in schools contain anecdotes of just such moments.

So how can we hold on to this new-dawn alertness as we walk through the lifelong day? How can we as adult Christians recapture that sense of awe and wonder, become like children, as our Lord commands, and enter the kingdom of heaven?

In recent years, many of us who work with children have been deeply influenced by an imaginative approach to Bible stories known as Godly Play. With its roots in the educational methodology of the Montessori tradition, Godly Play offers reflective presentations of scripture that help both old and young to fall in love with the story again. Through the use of carefully chosen and beautiful 3D figures, and working from scripts that have been tested over many years, groups are invited to experience Bible stories with plenty of space between the words and a reverence in the telling that can enable an encounter with God through the story as if it was being heard for the first time.

Like little children, we can hear these stories speaking to us with the freshness of a new day, even though we may well have read them many times before. This has been our experience again and again in the *Barnabas* team when using Godly Play in a variety of situations, including with adults on training days and with children in classrooms or holiday clubs.

Play is foundational to all good learning. The educationalist Froebel once described it as 'the purest, most spiritual activity... It gives... joy, freedom, contentment, inner and outer rest, peace with the world. It holds the sources of all that is good' (*On the Education of Man*, 1826). Sociological and psychological research backs up this claim. It is through play that we can discover and internalize deep learning for ourselves.

This is how we learn in the morning of our lives and, despite the lectures and literature that tend to define our adult education, it is nevertheless the way we learn best. This is surely why Jesus challenges us to remain childlike in our faith, because, of all truths, the truths of God can only be learned this way. Contrary to the popular maxim, we don't stop playing because we grow old; we grow old because we stop playing.

Godly Play offers a model of faith nurture but allows us to continue to play with the stories of God like a child. The objects and props used are indeed the 'language' of the nursery but they allow us to explore concepts and make connections in sensory ways. These are elements of good learning, which are too easily put aside as we grow up. We are taught to sit 'under the word' in neat lines in a church, as opposed to sitting in the midst of the word in creative circles, which is a feature of Godly Play.

Slowing a story down and setting the imagination free are not, of course, new ideas. Ignatian exercises encourage a similar approach, as does *lectio divina*—which is, arguably, what Godly Play introduces to children. What Godly Play adds, however, is the visual and tactile elements that stimulate the imagination. It turns words into 'flesh', and all this is experienced in the context of worship.

People sit in a community circle of believers; there is a built-in opportunity for a creative response, and this flows naturally into prayer together and a 'feast' that celebrates that togetherness.

For over four years now, I have been using this approach with the children of my own church in east London. Each Sunday I set up a 'classroom', surrounded by the 3D stories. There is a focal table holding models of the key elements of our faith—a nativity scene, a cross and a resurrection picture of Christ, flanked either side by a candle for Jesus as the light of the world and a model of the good shepherd with his sheep. It has been exciting and moving as the children I work with have demonstrated that they have picked up these unspoken messages of our belief and have related them to the other stories, which are arranged systematically on either side of the table.

Over my years of working with children's groups, I have used many programmes and styles, and I continue to do so in my work with schools and in special events with children, but I can honestly say that when it comes to nurturing the faith of children week by

week, Godly Play has reached deeper places in their young lives than I have ever observed before.

Godly Play allows stories from the Bible to breathe for themselves rather than being stifled by rigid learning outcomes and predetermined teaching points. I can understand that the latter may well be the stuff of a national

> ## We don't stop playing because we grow old; we grow old because we stop playing

curriculum but they may have little to do with a spiritual one. Godly Play also honours each child as a spiritually alive participant in the learning. It enables the early-morning clarity of children— their innate spirituality—to flourish as they make connections for themselves between God's story and their own.

It is widely agreed that what happens to us in the early years of our lives is highly influential and can set us on either firm or unstable paths that affect our whole future. In a similar way, our first encounters with scripture and the truths of God cannot come too early, and must surely be as positive an experience as possible. They should be encounters that invite us to hold on to and build on the childlike wonder that we have in the morning of our lives—a wonder at the depth and riches of what God is saying to us and the amazing truth that God wants to listen to what we have to say to him.

I have been reading *The Road to Emmaus* by Helen Julian CSF (BRF, 2007), in which one section focuses on Thomas Traherne. Here was a man who had not lost touch with his morning delight at hearing God's voice and held on to that wonder throughout his life. He writes, 'The pure and unsullied perception I had from the womb and that divine light with which I was born are to this day the best in which I can see the universe. By the gift of God they attended me into the world and by his especial favour I remember them still' (quoted in *The Wisdom of the English Mystics* by Robert Way, Sheldon Press, 1978).

The rediscovery of this early morning freshness in our walk with God can enable us to hear God's song throughout the day, and I believe that Godly Play is an exciting tool to experience this freshness, whatever time of day it is for us. ■

 You can read more about Godly Play on the *Barnabas* website: **www.barnabasinchurches.org.uk**. Or you can visit the official Godly Play site: www.godlyplay.org.uk.

The people

who touch the sky

'The Hands and Feet of Jesus' by Clive Price (BRF, 2007) shares the extraordinary stories of ordinary people expressing God's love in desperate and desolate places around the world. Published in conjunction with World Vision, it shows how strong faith combined with practical compassion can change lives. This abridged extract tells how one man in Bolivia realized that the dramatic results of development work outweigh the demands of just getting the job done.

L

Sleeping under the stars on a clay-brick bed with animal skins for sheets, he wondered if he had made the right career move. 'What am I doing here?'

Marcos Quino thought to himself. 'Did I study that much for this? If my family gets to know about this, they will mock me. As soon as I get back, I'll quit.'

Marcos had only just started at World Vision's field office in Bolivia. His first trip had been to Laja, a town in the middle of the cold, high plains of the Altiplano. Parts of the region are rocky and barren, almost like a Martian landscape. When he left this desolate place three days later, he wrote his resignation letter:

…to give them an active role in their fight against poverty

It turned out to be an inhospitable place for him, and he pleaded to be moved

I talked to the National Director. He explained to me in more detail what the job was all about, what World Vision was all about—and that moved my heart. I never gave her my letter.

It was my duty as a professional to serve these people… we had opportunities they never had, so it was only fair to help them get the opportunities they needed. So I stayed.

Marcos was born in Oruro, north-east Bolivia. Formerly a busy centre in the 1940s and 1950s, thanks to silver extraction, now it can look like a ghost town. Only the February carnival breaks up the monotony. Normally it's a passing-through place where miners get their supplies and then return home…

As a young teenager, Marcos had heard about World Vision. In 1984, he found out that there was a vacancy at their Bolivian field office. Almost at the same time, there was an opening at the Bolivian Central Bank that interested him, so he applied for that one, too. Both institutions offered him jobs.

It was a dilemma. Marcos liked both placements, but his father helped him to discern the right way forward: go with a stable Christian organization that was serving the poor, or with an unstable financial institution with better money. Convincing himself that 'money isn't everything', Marcos decided to work with World Vision. One of his first tasks was to serve with a project in Laja—an assignment that almost put him off relief and development work for life.

His next position was as Projects Promoter in Oruro. His team thought it would be a treat for him to return to his home town, but Marcos had only been born there and had never actually lived as part of the community. It turned out to be an inhospitable place for him, and he pleaded to be moved somewhere else.

Three months later, he was given responsibility for projects in La Paz and Pando, on the borderlands with Brazil. He enjoyed increased freedom and worked in the area for two years. Eventually Marcos became National Manager:

That [job] was made for me. I could really do what I wanted to do now.

I felt uplifted and useful again. I got to know all the projects in the country and that enhanced my point of view.

I always gave my 100 per cent in all the positions I was in. And that was acknowledged by the institution — which was great for me — because my dream was always to give the best I could in everything.

Marcos has benefited in more ways than one by working with World Vision. He met a nutritionist and dietician called Esther, who had visited one of the projects as part of a church group. She later became his wife, and supports him in his role.

Marcos has made some remarkable inroads. In Santa Cruz, a community leader rose up in opposition against World Vision. In a bid to become involved—and potentially close down the work from the inside—he climbed to the dizzy heights of becoming president of the board of one of the projects. Ironically, he became one of World Vision's best spokesmen, and even made a personal commitment to the Christian faith. 'He could have easily destroyed us if he'd wanted,' says Marcos, 'but he changed to become our best ally.'

In 1998, Marcos' team arranged for twelve classrooms to be built for a community on the outskirts of Santa Cruz. The project made a great difference for children who used to attend schools located far away (which had put many at risk).

Marcos believes that, like any organization, World Vision has had its ups and downs. Yet it has always maintained its Christian identity:

It has brought a social consciousness to the church. It has helped, by its own experience, to guide the church to this change from the temple to the community.

It has a different speech and different focus. Many NGOs do similar things, but World Vision has a biblical perspective. It's all about empowering the communities, to give them an active role in their fight against poverty.

He feels that the organization's work has resulted in transformation. Indeed, he refers to World Vision as 'a school of change'. The Bolivian team may not have reached 'multitudes' but, in his

---

The project made a great difference for children who used to attend schools located far away

---

humble words, they have reached 'a few children'—and, as Marcos puts it, 'that will make a difference'.

Being a leader in development work is not easy. 'When I stay home for more than two weeks in a row,' says Marcos, 'my son and daughter ask me, "Why aren't you travelling this week?" So far I've been with World Vision for more than 20 years. And if God wants me to, I'll stay with them longer.' ∎

Music for the soul:
the sound of sunrise

Gordon Giles is vicar of St Mary Magdalene's Church, Enfield, north London. He contributes to BRF's 'New Daylight' notes and has also written 'The Music of Praise' (2002), 'The Harmony of Heaven' (2003) and 'O Come, Emmanuel' (2005) for BRF.

Sunrise has inspired various composers to attempt to describe it musically.

There is nothing more beautiful than sunrise. For many, it is a natural work of art, a daily reminder (if you are up!) that once again God has bestowed goodness and beauty on the earth. Sunrise is actually an atmospheric refraction of light from the sun while it is, technically speaking, still over the edge of the horizon, by which those wonderful dissipations of red, orange and yellow are stretched across the canvas of the sky—a cosmological masterpiece. However we attempt to describe sunrise, though, it is also a temporary phenomenon. After a few minutes it is gone and the sun is up. 'Morning has broken,' as Eleanor Farjeon put it in that famous hymn, 'like the first morning'.

I am the Lord, and there is no other; besides me there is no god. I arm you, though you do not know me, so that they may know, from the rising of the sun and from the west, that there is no one besides me; I am the Lord, and there is no other. I form light and create darkness, I make weal and create woe; I the Lord do all these things. Shower, O heavens, from above, and let the skies rain down righteousness; let the earth open, that salvation may spring up, and let it cause righteousness to sprout up also; I the Lord have created it.

ISAIAH 45:5–8 (NRSV)

Sunrise has inspired various composers to attempt to describe it musically. One of the most famous examples comes from *The Creation*, an oratorio written in 1798 by Joseph Haydn (1732–1809), in which the inspiration comes from *Paradise Lost* by the 17th-century poet John Milton:

In splendour bright is rising now
the sun and darts his rays;
an am'rous joyful happy spouse,
a giant proud and glad
to run his measured course.

Haydn had tried portraying a sunrise before, in his 6th symphony, written soon after his employment by the Prince of Eszterházy, in the spring of 1761. The symphony, which contains many virtuosic sections for each member of the orchestra, was warmly received by Haydn's new employer, and was soon nicknamed 'Le Matin', undoubtedly because of the opening notes, which attempt to illustrate a sunrise in music.

Once again God has bestowed **goodness and beauty on the earth**

> Sunrise is actually an atmospheric refraction of light from the sun

... his unsung songs, his unmade works, his unwept tears and his unasked questions

At the dawn of the 20th century, Maurice Ravel composed a marvellous 'sunrise' for his ballet *Daphnis and Chloe*, as did Arnold Schoenberg (1874–1951) in his song cycle *Gurre-Lieder*. More famously, perhaps, there is Edvard Grieg's 'Morning mood' (*Morgenstemning*), often just called 'Morning', from the incidental music he wrote for his friend Henrik Ibsen's play *Peer Gynt*, composed between 1874 and 1875. In a wonderful evocation of a Scandinavian dawn, the flute plays a lyrical repeated theme, which builds up as the sun's rays penetrate the cold darkness. There is a spiritual easing in the placing of this piece in the play's action, for it comes after the death of Peer's mother, Åse. Then comes the even more famous passage 'In the hall of the mountain king', where Peer is invited to marry the troll-king's daughter. The doom and gloom are lifted by the charming melody of the flute, announcing a new dawn, a hope after death, and strength to go on, lit by sunlight.

The plot of *Peer Gynt* is rather convoluted, telling the tale of an anti-hero who disgraces himself at a wedding in the presence of an eminent Norwegian Lutheran, whose daughter Solveig he falls for. It is a fantasy play in which Peer, who claims to have been both a missionary and a slave trader, travels widely, having conversations with the sphinx, pretending to be a Bedouin, and ultimately falling in with the local madmen, who hail him as a prophet. He concludes that everyone lives in a world of their own and ends up being hailed as 'Emperor of the Self'. Peer becomes demented himself and calls upon the 'keeper of all fools'—that is, on God—to save him.

Eventually he leaves and, on his homeward journey, meets a strange passenger who wants to use his body to discover where dreams emanate from. Peer is shipwrecked and miserable but gets home, only to find himself at a funeral and then an auction, at which he is confronted with all that he didn't do—his unsung songs, his unmade works, his unwept tears and his unasked questions. Then, as the play concludes, he is told that his wicked soul must be melted down unless he can account for himself.

Peer seeks a priest but meets the devil instead, who decides that, in fact, Peer is not quite wicked enough to go to hell. Peer realizes that he is nothing and has done nothing with his life, but as he reaches the point of despair, good and pure Solveig sings, and his inner voice tells him to 'turn around'. His soul is still in peril but he asks Solveig to give account for his sins, and she tells him that he has none to confess now. Confused, Peer asks, 'Where was I as the one I should have been, whole and true, with the mark of God on my brow?' She replies, 'In my faith, in my hope, in my love', echoing Paul's first letter to the Corinthians (13:13). Peer then collapses into her arms as this strange drama about choice and fate, sin and redemption, darkness and light, night and day, draws to an end.

Next time you listen to 'Morning mood', spare a thought for Peer Gynt, who represents us all in our journey through life as we encounter and attempt to resist temptation, making choices for which we must take responsibility, not only in this world but in the next. And remember the beautiful Solveig, whose final role in the play reminds us of Christ, who cancels our sin, having opened up new life on the other side of death on that joyous Easter morning. ■

> ... Christ, who cancels our sin, having opened up new life on the other side of death

Readings for reflection

Genesis 1:1–5
1 Corinthians 13

Music to listen to

'Morning mood' from *Peer Gynt* by Edvard Grieg. There are many recordings available. Try *Aurora: Music of the Northern Lights* released by Deutsche Gramophon (ref: DG 471 747-2) in 2002, played by the Goteborgs Symfoniker, conducted by Neeme Järvi.

New every morning:
the life behind a favourite hymn

Emma Garrow works as a freelance writer. She is a member of the South West Spiritual Directors' Network and volunteers with a hospital chaplaincy visiting team.

'Great is thy faithfulness' is an all-time favourite hymn. Its heartening sentiments and joyful tune inspire congregations to praise, and it is certainly a hymn I love to sing. Proclaiming its sure statement of God's goodness can be faith-enhancing.

Sometimes, though, I find myself questioning the words of the chorus even while singing it: 'Morning by morning new mercies I see'. I wonder at the obvious lack of mercies in the world and the places where I feel a lack in my own life. I wonder whether it is some blindness of my own that makes these mercies at times appear invisible. Could it be that the words of the chorus, 'All I have needed Thy hand hath provided', are a promise requiring patience? Yet the hymn is the song of one who has already experienced fulfilment. Can he have been alone in that?

Each morning's new mercies could count as the things we see in nature—the rising sun, the dawn chorus, the spring daffodil or summer rose. They could count as the smell of coffee or the sound of a child laughing downstairs.

Yet we all know that in some dark corners of the world there are no flowers and no morning breakfast. In our own lives we may find ourselves alone. So what is it that God's hand has provided for us?

The mornings of Thomas Chisholm

'Great is thy faithfulness' is a very personal hymn. In it, the author, Thomas Chisholm, speaks of his own experience of God. Like the seasons and heavens of his verse, he 'joins with all nature' to testify to God's faithfulness. Yet in relating his own experience to that of the whole earth's, he also draws a general conclusion about the universal availability of God's goodness.

It is not until we reach the last verse that we realize what Chisholm counts as God's blessings of fulfilment: not a perfect life, neither children nor a spouse, neither good health nor a pleasant green land to abide in, but 'pardon for sin', 'strength for today', 'bright hope for tomorrow'.

Chisholm took part of his inspiration from the Old Testament book of Lamentations: 'The steadfast love of the Lord never ceases, his mercies never come to an end; they are new every morning; great is your faithfulness. "The Lord is my portion," says my soul, "therefore I will hope in him"' (3:22–24, NRSV).

These verses recognize that God himself is the fulfilment of our needs. It is in the act of bringing all the elements of our lives, both joys and griefs, to the place where we wait for God, that we find he can meet the needs and fill the gaps.

So who was Thomas Chisholm and what kind of experiences did he have to prompt him to write this hymn?

> **The experiences from which he wrote are more of the ordinary, everyday kind**

Pardon for sin, strength for today, **bright hope for tomorrow**

Chisholm was an American writer, the author of over 1200 poems. He wrote 'Great is thy faithfulness' in 1923, when he was 57 years old, and sent it to the Moody Bible Institute in Chicago, where a musician, William Runyan, put it to music.

It is tempting to imagine that there must be a great story behind Chisholm's words, some disaster out of which he felt lifted by God and inspired to tell the tale for the rest of his life. But the experiences from which he wrote are more of the ordinary, everyday kind, albeit in a different time and place.

Chisholm was born in 1866 in a log cabin in Kentucky, USA. He began working as a school teacher when he

was 16, in the school where he had received his own education. As a young man, he attended a revival meeting and became a committed

We can only imagine...

Christian. He was ordained into the Methodist Church but, after only a short time in his new role, ill health forced him to resign. He later worked as a life insurance agent in Indiana. Though he lived to the age of 94, the ill health that had robbed him of his ministerial work was a persistent feature of his life.

We can only imagine the kind of questions Chisholm must have had on losing his role in the Church. These days, we place a high value on living out our dreams, and an inability to do that can feel like failure. A letter Chisholm wrote in 1941, aged 75, records his own response. He said, 'My income has not been large at any time due to impaired health, but I must not fail to record here the unfailing faithfulness of a covenant-keeping God, for which I am filled with astonishing gratefulness.'

Chisholm felt that on his conversion he had entered into a covenant with God, which, despite some unfortunate turns to his life, God had kept. Through his poetry he found a new vocation, and through his personal experience of God's faithfulness he bequeathed a story and a hymn to encourage the faith of generations to come. When he wrote, 'Morning by morning new mercies I see', he was writing what he had found to be true.

Our mornings

When my husband and I moved from the area where we had spent our whole married life thus far, we were ready for new opportunities. But while he was going to a new job, I was yet to discover what the move would mean for me. A phrase delivered by a friend captured my imagination. She said that she hoped I would be open to whatever God wanted to give me in my new home.

The phrase lingered because it was the reverse of how I had been thinking until then. I had been imagining that I must discover what God wanted me to do for him in the new place. The idea that God wanted to give to me, and that this was what I could be looking out for, seemed brazen but liberating.

Shortly after we moved, we received a postcard, a photograph of a blue-and-white rowing boat on the water. The image somehow fitted together with the words I had heard. I saw myself, not just in the big move to an unfamiliar part of the country, but every morning, pushing my boat out into the water, setting off with a readiness to discover whatever God wanted to give me each day.

As time passed and we settled into our new home, I discovered new friends and activities and found, after a while, that I could trace the blessings that had begun with an encouragement to be open to God's gifts.

God himself is the **fulfilment** of our needs

Another new morning

Thomas Chisholm lived a life in which expectation gave way to disappointment, and status, good health and prosperity met their limits. Yet he had a perspective on his days that enabled him to sing of God's love throughout his long years. His great hymn and the words of Lamentations are an encouragement that God makes his love known in all our days, no matter what they bring or fail to bring, by offering relationship with him as his greatest gift. Looking at his life from within this relationship, Chisholm was able to make out God's mercies every morning, and to count God's presence as the best of blessings in each new day. ■

A prayer for each morning:

Lord, help me to be open to what you want to give me today.

When morning never comes

Lisa Cherrett is BRF's Project Editor and Managing Editor for Bible reading notes publishing. She has also written 'The Triumph of Goodness: biblical themes in the Harry Potter stories' (BRF, 2003).

'Weeping may linger for the night, but joy comes with the morning' (Psalm 30:5, NRSV). So says the psalmist, King David, with enviable confidence. But for some of us, sometimes, that morning can seem a very long time coming. We may not feel so joyful when we hear the dawn chorus, see the sky brightening outside our window, and have to face another challenging day after another sleepless night. Or maybe our first waking moments bring the heavy, sickening consciousness of an ongoing grief that seems insoluble—a hopeless love, a bereavement or a suffering relative or friend.

At times like these, we may feel like King David in a different mood. Faced with the 'terrors of death', David let out an agonized plea: 'O that I had wings like a dove! I would fly away and be at rest; truly, I would flee far away' (Psalm 55:6–7).

Escape—it certainly seems an inviting prospect when that joyful morning never seems to come. 'Why are you putting me through this, Lord? Just let me off the hook!' But in my experience, escape is rarely what the Lord has in mind.

I suffer from occasional insomnia. It usually happens the night before I have to drive somewhere different from my usual routine commute, and I usually try to make sure I've got alternatives to fall back on: I look up the possibility of public transport, or I ask my husband if he'd be able to drive me—and I try to make sure I don't have any additional stresses, like a very early start or extra responsibilities that would mean letting others down if I fail to turn up. I call them my 'escape routes', and if they're in place I usually manage at least some sleep. But it's amazing how often my carefully laid plans fall apart one by one, leaving me with the single option of simply trusting God for today and leaving tomorrow in his hands.

In my early 20s, I spent five years in a heartbreaking relationship of unrequited love. The easiest solution, and the one most people would have advised had I asked them, would have been to cut off the friendship and escape the pain. But I was convinced that this was not God's way, that I had to walk with him, through the experience and out at the other end. There was nothing I could do to change the circumstances—only hold on to God.

When morning is a long way off, and God is not allowing us to escape from the darkness, we may have to cope differently, depending on where God is in the situation. Does he seem close at hand or distant? Is he speaking to us or is he inexplicably, frustratingly silent? If we can hear God speaking, the response is relatively easy: we listen, trust and follow. Even if his words to us are not what we want to hear, we at least have the comfort of knowing that he's still involved and interested. His clear voice and felt presence brought me through the pain of my hopeless love.

He may be silent, though. There's a name for that

Is he speaking to us or is he inexplicably, **frustratingly silent?**

---

alternative—the 'dark night of the soul'—and it can last a very long time. 'If God seems a long way off, it must be you who moved' is a simplistic, guilt-inducing little saying that may be nowhere near the truth. When God seems to absent himself—often coinciding with some kind of life change or emotional trauma (but not as the result of unconfessed sin)—our faith can go through a phase of being dismantled piece by piece, until we are left with the very barest bones, perhaps just one thing we know to be true about God or our relationship with him.

In the dark night of the soul, the words of another Psalm ring true: 'My soul thirsts for God, for the living God. When shall I come and behold the face of God? My tears have been my food day and night, while people say to me continually, "Where is your God?"' (Psalm 42:2–3). Tears day *and* night: no 'joy in the morning' here. This is, at least at first, a fearful and angry time.

There are, perhaps, three things to do during those dark days and nights.

God's grace makes up the shortfall in our own capacities

- Keep talking to God, even though he doesn't talk back. If you feel like it, shout. He doesn't mind hearing honest rage.
- Keep trusting God, even in the anger and fear. Hold on to the one thing you know to be true about him and stay free of bitterness.
- Keep trying to tune in to God. When the 'dark night of the soul' ends, you may find that you hear God on a different 'frequency' from before, so to speak. New, different forms of prayer and worship may bring a deeper awareness of his presence. It is almost as though he has to switch off one transmitter for a time, before he can turn on another.

If escape is not an option during the long night of tears, what is the alternative? It is just to wait. Everything in us may rebel against that idea. Waiting sounds passive, a waste of precious time, a waste of life. Yet, strange as it may seem, waiting can be an active, dynamic thing to do. Waiting and watching for God to act in response to our prayers can build patience, confidence, and attentiveness to his voice. Waiting through the sense of panic and the urge to 'flee far away' can breed fearlessness and knowledge of the peace and strength that God's Spirit can bring. Waiting in the full awareness of our inability to solve all our problems can blossom in a new experience of God's grace, which makes up the shortfall in our own capacities.

Yet again, a psalmist says it best: 'I wait for the Lord, my soul waits, and in his word I put my hope. My soul waits for the Lord more than watchmen wait for the morning, more than watchmen wait for the morning' (Psalm 130:5–6, NIV).

Night-time may seem to be everlasting and overwhelming, but morning does come at last. ∎

I know you

I know you
in the first, faint flare of dawn
when trees stand, hushed and black,
against the yellowing blue.

I know you
in the glory of the sun
bursting the horizon,
chasing the night,
discovering colour.

I know you
in the rising breeze,
the rustle of leaves,
the slink of home-returning cats,
the busy flit of little birds
about their breakfast.

In this daily miracle of loving sustenance,
this morning of the world,
I know you,
Lord.

And so,
in this intended re-creation,
this new awakening,
this little, daily resurrection
I sense the promise
of another, greater, personal,
of fullest knowing,
of longing love fulfilled.

FRANCIS BUXTON

Learning to love

The work of the Romance Academy

Jason Gardner works for the London Institute for Contemporary Christianity as a Youth Project Researcher, and for Romance Academy as a Development Manager. He is married to RA's creative director, Rachel.

One of the most frequent criticisms of today's society is that people's interaction with technology simply doesn't allow them time or space to reflect. Take, for instance, the experiment conducted in Washington DC earlier in 2007, when world-class violinist Joshua Bell, playing a £2million violin, busked in a Metro station during rush hour. Only two people actually stopped to listen to him play during the 45 minutes he spent there. Most of the commuting crowd were completely unaware that they were listening to some of the most beautiful music in the world: they were talking on the phone, focused on getting to work or, as one commuter

Young people often have low expectations of sex

attested, listening to Brit Goth band The Cure on their iPod.

For today's teenagers, the word 'reflect' rarely appears in their day-to-day existence except in the occasional essay question. Their world is a non-stop buzz of pop music, soaps, school and, most importantly for them, good times with friends. So when it comes to getting them to think about a really vital area of their lives, such as sex and relationships, how do we create a space for them in which they're comfortable, where they can learn about and, most importantly, reflect upon not simply what they want out of relationships but what makes a healthy relationship?

This is really the heart of Romance Academy. It presents an opportunity not to preach at young people about what they should or shouldn't be doing but to help them get to grips with a topic that is one of the key factors influencing their future happiness.

By now you may be wondering what a Romance Academy looks like. Allow me to oblige. Twelve young people—six boys, six girls—embark on a 16-week course of close mentoring by two trained youth workers.

At the initial stage of the project, they're encouraged to sign a 'pledge' to stop sexual activity for the duration of the course (which doesn't mean, of course, that all participants are already sexually active). This is designed to give them space to reflect on their own, each other's and society's attitude to relationships and sex.

Each week they meet as the leaders provide input and provoke peer-generated discussion on different aspects of love and relationships: the physical and emotional impact of having sex; how to grow beyond relationships built purely on sexual attraction and activity; how to respect members of the opposite sex; how use of drugs and alcohol impacts not just our ability to make right choices but also our ability to form right relationships.

There are extra-curricular activities aimed at

> By now you may be wondering what a Romance Academy looks like. Allow me to oblige…

enhancing group cohesion and introducing the participants to different ways of relating to each other. For instance, we offer an activity-based weekend away, salsa lessons, ice skating, and a 'date' night on which they learn dating etiquette.

We also encourage them to think seriously about the consequences of their decisions, as well as pointing out the benefits of mutual support in a relationship. For example, for one weekend the young people have to 'pair off' and look after an electronic 'baby' for the weekend.

The course ends in a graduation ceremony. The Romance Academy graduates, along with their friends and family, celebrate all they've learnt on the course and receive a certificate noting their achievement.

The very first Romance Academy was filmed as a documentary for BBC2 entitled *No Sex Please, We're Teenagers*. The youth workers involved were Dan Burke and my wife Rachel Gardner. The series caused such a stir when it was aired in autumn 2005 that, since then, the RA team have been darting up and down the country training youth workers to run Academies in their own areas.

So does it work? Well, whenever you ask that question you have to define what you mean by success, but I think the following quote from one of the first 'graduates'—Grace, then 16 years old—sums up a lot of what the project achieves:

I had never known what I really wanted in relationships. I lost my virginity when I was 14, and had slept with two different boys. When I heard about the Romance Academy, I knew I wanted to explore more about relationships...Being in the Romance Academy gave me the confidence to say I wanted to wait [for sex in her new relationship]. Before, I would have jumped in and had sex straight away, but I gave myself time, and we really got to know each other. Everything I learnt through the Academy helped me to become a sort of grown-up. I was so naïve before. I have learnt that I can be loved and I can now love myself, I don't have to do things to be loved.

What makes a healthy relationship?

The benefits of mutual support

Success, for us, doesn't simply mean that young people become abstinent or delay sexual activity. What we've experienced is that Romance Academy gives young people a better understanding of who they are, and improves their self-confidence and social skills. Many of the graduates and their families have attested to the way it has helped to improve relationships at home as well. Providing them with a safe space, with the support of peers, means that they understand what it means to have a better relationship, not just one-on-one with a partner but also with their networks of friends and family.

> **... completely unaware that they were listening to some of the most beautiful music in the world**

'Everything I learnt through the Academy helped me to become a sort of grown-up'

Key to our development of Romance Academy has been a recognition that we need to start where young people are and journey with them for a while, rather than being solely focused on where we want them to end up. So we're acutely conscious of the many pressures placed on them to fit in with their peers and with society's expectations. In today's world, it's hard not to associate success and happiness with being sexually desirable. Obviously that's a very superficial approach to any understanding of human worth but it's one that is prevalent. The knock-on effect is young people with low self-esteem, who feel that having sex in some way means that they're wanted and accepted—even if only for a short while.

As sex dominates our world so much, the flipside is that young people often have low expectations of sex. It's just another experience to fit in after getting stoned or drunk at a party. Sometimes sex happens more out of boredom than a need to be desired.

Romance Academy speaks into this world. We start with an understanding that teenagers are influenced by four key areas: family, friends, school and media. When it comes to decision-making for young people, all those factors come into play. Although a 14-year-old might tell you that what matters most to them is the opinion of their friends, certainly media and family also play a big part in the choices they make—even if those choices are an act of defiance against family expectations. So we try to improve their understanding of their families and of how the media represent sex, all the while ensuring that we don't just teach them but that they teach each other in how they listen and interact with the questions we give them.

Ultimately we want to bring another influence to bear: faith and spirituality. We don't demand that Romance Academy leaders should be Christians but we do ask them to respect the fact that the organization is founded on Christian principles and a Christian ethos.

For the Christians involved in Romance Academy, having a Christian ethos means exploring what God was playing at when he made male and female in his image (Genesis 1:27). It's about understanding the complementary nature of relationships between the sexes. God places humans within a paradise in Eden—a context designed to help them flourish, not simply survive. God creates man for woman and woman for man, in order that each one can grow through relationship and assist the other in completing the all-important task of doing God's will.

We hope to stir up in young people a sense of longing—the sense that there must be more to sex than society says, because God invested it with such a deep purpose. It's been our privilege to help youth workers help young people to begin to connect with some of their God-given abilities and their own inherent worth.

What we love about Romance Academy is that in helping young people to reflect on what makes life and love really valuable, we're helping them to pick out, amid the demands and pressures of life, some extraordinarily beautiful music. ∎

It's hard not to associate success and happiness with being sexually desirable

Ultimately we want to bring another influence to bear: **faith and spirituality**

Amy Carmichael:
labouring from dawn till dusk

Heather Coupland loves working alongside her husband, who is a vicar in Surrey. She enjoys writing about everyday spirituality and is a contributor to CWR's 'Inspiring Women Every Day' Bible reading notes.

Make us Thy labourers,
Let us not dream of ever looking back,
Let not our knees be feeble, hands be slack,
O make us strong to labour, strong to bear,
From the rising of the morning till the
stars appear.

This verse from one of Amy Carmichael's many poems gives us an insight into the attitude to serving God that pervaded the whole life of this extraordinary missionary. She was born into a devout Christian family on 16 December 1867 in Northern Ireland and died in India on 18 January 1951, having served the Christian fellowship she established in Dohnavur for over 50 years.

Amy was the eldest of seven children and enjoyed a very happy childhood in which faith in God played a large part. One evening, when she was three years old, she prayed with great faith that God would change the colour of her eyes from brown to blue, as she thought blue a much prettier colour. On waking the following morning, she pulled a chair to the dressing table in order to see the exciting results of her prayer in the mirror. At first she was bewildered on seeing the same brown eyes looking back at her, but after a while she felt the words 'Isn't "No" an answer?' come into her mind. Whether this was the whisper of God's Spirit or whether she had heard her mother say something similar, we do not know, but this was a lesson that stayed with her throughout her life.

She was a very adventurous and energetic child, being the leader in many pranks with her siblings, once suggesting that they see how many laburnum pods they could eat before they died! Fortunately their mother discovered what had happened and was able to give them some rather disgusting medicine that prevented any ill effects.

As a young adult, Amy was greatly influenced by the teaching from the early Keswick Conventions. In 1887 she heard Hudson Taylor speak about the 'plight of the lost' and wrote, 'Does it not stir up our hearts to go forth and help them, does it not make us long to leave our exceeding abundant life and go to them that sit in darkness?' And so the seeds of a desire to be a missionary were sown.

Five years later, those seeds germinated when, as she was praying, she felt the Lord speak the words 'Go ye' simply but powerfully into her heart. The destination was unclear but the call was unmistakable and Amy set out to discover where she should go. She spent a fruitful time in Japan and Ceylon before settling in India in 1895 and staying there until the end of her life.

It's easy for us today to look back at Victorian missionaries with a feeling of embarrassment or discomfort as we see them attempting to forge an outpost of the Empire in a foreign country. Amy Carmichael was indeed one such Victorian ambassador for

> ... a prolific ministry of writing letters and notes of **encouragement**

Christ and yet she was also a true radical. She wore a sari (even if it was accompanied by a pith helmet!) and often stained her hands and face with coffee so that she could travel to remote villages unobserved. She learned Tamil and longed to recruit co-workers from among the local people, which was unusual in those days.

Her passion was to rescue babies and young girls from being dedicated to Hindu temple gods. These young girls were being sold into drudgery, exploitation and prostitution at the very beginning of their lives. Amy discovered that her rescue work could be dangerous, as she was often threatened when angry templegoers, who wanted to buy the children, gathered round her bungalow. The first baby girl was rescued in 1904 and the work grew rapidly. By 1913 the family in Dohnavur numbered 140 females and by 1952 the work had expanded to include boys as well. This meant that there were over 900 people living in community together.

The children lived in nurseries with their carers and were expected to help with practical tasks as well as receiving a basic education. Having fun was important to Amy and she

Having fun was important to Amy and she would teach the children many songs

would teach the children many songs, both educational and spiritual. She also enjoyed it when groups of them came to her room simply to play and spend time with her. This obviously became more difficult as numbers grew but she still wanted to be there as a mother to them. She tried to keep in contact with each child and co-worker through regular meetings and through a prolific ministry of writing letters and notes of encouragement. Many of the children remained working within the family at Dohnavur into adulthood.

In September 1931, the circumstances of her life took another turn when she slipped and fell, breaking her leg and dislocating her ankle. Everyone presumed she would soon be back to full strength, but full physical healing never came and for 20 years she remained an invalid who rarely left her room. This was not the end of her influential ministry, however, either in India or further afield. She wrote 13 books and continued to be in close contact with many members of the Christian family she had established in Dohnavur, except when severe pain or fatigue dictated otherwise.

Amy Carmichael poured out her life for others as she offered herself in love and service to God, and I have been hugely inspired and challenged as I have read about her. She listened for the voice of God and, when she heard it, she stepped out in faith and impacted the lives of many, many people. At the beginning of her ministry in India, an old man came to her and said, 'We have heard much preaching. Can you show us the life of the Lord Jesus?' His question inspired her to try to show people Jesus through the way that she lived her life, and, over 100 years later, her life inspires me to want to do the same. ■

Ashburnham Place:

a place
of blessing

Andrew Wooding Jones is an ordained Anglican who, after training in hotel management, studying at Oak Hill theological college, a curacy in south-east London and six years as Associate Rector and Director of Pastoral Care at St Thomas Crookes, Sheffield, was appointed Resident Director of Ashburnham Place in 2000.

... a place of God's peace

These words from the prophet Haggai have had great relevance to the work of the Ashburnham Christian Trust in Ashburnham Place ever since they inspired the Revd John Bickersteth to convert the former stately home he had inherited into a Christian prayer and conference centre.

'The glory of this present house will be greater than the glory of the former house,' says the Lord Almighty. 'And in this place I will grant peace,' declares the Lord Almighty.

HAGGAI 2:9 (NIV)

Since the trust was established in 1960, thousands of people have visited Ashburnham Place, as members of church groups or as individuals joining organized events or staying in the Prayer Centre. The visitors have included Christians from around the world attending international conferences or serving as volunteers, and local people visiting the grounds and gardens, using the conference centre for local meetings and praying in the Prayer Centre for the local area.

Ashburnham Place is a prayer and conference centre situated in East Sussex, near Hastings and Eastbourne and just outside Battle, the site of the Battle of Hastings. That describes the 'headlines' but not only is there so much more to it than that, we believe there is much more to come.

I moved to Ashburnham in 2000, coming with my wife Margaret from Sheffield, where we had been part of the leadership team at St Thomas Crookes Church. Together we became only the third set of leaders of Ashburnham Christian Trust since it began, and we felt, with the Trustees, that this was already a place where many people had received blessing. We also felt that it was to become known as 'A place of blessing', and this has become the Trust's mission statement.

Drawing on Mike Breen's book *A Passionate Life* (Kingsway, 2005), we came up with the concept of a triangle, balanced on two sides by 'guests' and 'team' and with God at the top. This was all about the challenge of balancing our lifestyle as staff to ensure that Ashburnham Place continued to fulfil its calling to be a place of God's glory and a place of God's peace.

Our prayer is that our guests will find God's blessing as they visit Ashburnham Place. We pray that they will discover that blessing whether or not they are people of Christian faith, so we also pray for those who are suppliers, those who deliver and those who come from local businesses and organizations to use the facilities, so that in this place and through our service they might encounter God.

As a staff team of nearly 80 from (currently) 24 nations and a variety of Christian backgrounds, many living on site and some off site, we pray that in our life as a Christian community we might extend blessing to each other. We know that as we seek to dwell in unity, we can pray that God will bestow blessing (Psalm 133).

As we feed our guests, clean and prepare their accommodation and maintain the buildings and grounds, we are aware that if we seek to bless

> ⌐ ... these volunteers have been part of a growing and **popular discipleship programme**

those who come as guests, they will be better able to meet with God. If our attitudes create a hindrance or obstacle, we will equally create a hindrance to that discovery of God's blessing, glory and peace.

If you arrive at Ashburnham Place on a Saturday, you will find residential and day groups using the centre from across the south-east of England. Guests use the former rooms of the stately home as meeting rooms for groups numbering from 200 and upwards down to 10–20. Accommodation is in buildings built more recently, with an increasing number of en suite rooms. As groups worship, pray and reflect on God's word, the staff team will have been praying that God will meet with them

... renewed, refreshed and resourced for a new week

and bless them as individuals and as church communities. As groups plan their programmes, they include time for sessions together, time to eat together but also time to enjoy the grounds and gardens.

The grounds and gardens are part of the unique character of Ashburnham Place. The mixture of woodland (some of it a Site of Special Scientific Interest), lakes, formal gardens, a prayer garden and open spaces used for ball games and larger camping events provides lots of opportunity to reflect and relax.

As well as the main conference centre, we also have the Prayer Centre, located in what were once the stables of the stately home. At the moment, this space is used by

individuals and small groups who take advantage of prayer rooms in the coach house and an extension in the grounds to meet with God in prayer.

Alongside church and Prayer Centre groups, Ashburnham Christian Trust runs a programme including events for men and for women, teaching events, creative breaks and Christian holidays. In the summer months, we host bigger events with groups such as *Salt and Light* and *Ichthus* running camps for up to 2000 people. Many are delighted to be able to choose between camping (doing their own cooking) and being able to sleep in a bed and have meals provided!

Ashburnham Place is much more than a facility for those who come to visit. Ever since the centre was first opened, it has benefited from the input of Christian volunteers from around the world. In recent years, these volunteers have been part of a growing and popular discipleship programme which has been designed to equip them to return to their nations better able to serve God in their generation. The group of volunteers is between 40 and 50 in number and they stay from six to twelve months. A small number may stay for a second year to develop skills in leadership.

Alongside the group of volunteers, there is a group of permanent staff. Many of these are exploring the vision that Ashburnham should be not only their place of work but also their place of Christian fellowship and spiritual belonging. Currently, all staff and volunteers meet each day at 10.30am to pray, worship and focus on God's word. We are aware of the enormous privilege it is to be able to pause in our daily work in this way but we know that we must keep God in the centre of all we do. Sometimes these meetings are with the whole community together, sometimes they are in smaller cell groups or departments.

On Sundays, around 70 people gather in the evening for a service. At the end of a busy weekend, these times allow the team to be renewed, refreshed and resourced for a new week. Every quarter we close to guests and have a Community Day, which allows space to meet with God and look forward to the ways in which God is leading us—as well as giving us a chance to have fun together. These days are always highlights in our life as community.

As we look forward, there are exciting challenges ahead for Ashburnham Place. In the 1970s the Prayer Centre ran a cycle of continuous prayer and we believe that God wants us to return to that call.

Having been involved in Prayer Week (www.prayerweek.com), in the Global Day of Prayer (www.globaldayofprayer.com) and having opened a creative prayer room with different zones to help people to be thankful, to pray for our area, the world, our community and its friends, and to express prayer using art, we feel that we are moving towards a time when the staff team will resource continuous prayer and worship that guests will be encouraged to join. This will include prayer for our region, nation and the nations of the world. Guests will still be able to visit Ashburnham Place to pursue their own call to prayer as well.

There are exciting challenges ahead for Ashburnham Place

We believe that we must be engaging more widely with the place where God has put us. We are excited to be able to support *Hope 08*, a national initiative encouraging Christians to be involved in mission in word and deed (www.hope08.com) and to be a resource to villages, towns and cities that are looking for support in prayer and in practical ways as they get involved. ■

More information about Ashburnham Place can be found at our website www.ashburnham.org.uk or by calling us on 01424 892244.

Morning

These prayers are written by Helen-Ann Hartley, who is a curate in the Wheatley Team Ministry near Oxford, and tutor in New Testament at Ripon College, Cuddesdon.

Above the tomb of the Venerable Bede in Durham Cathedral, there is an excerpt from his commentary on Revelation which reads, 'Christ is the Morning Star who when the night of this world is past brings to his saints the promise of the light of life and opens everlasting day.' Our prayers through the week echo this hope, reflecting on words from Psalm 139 (NRSV) that speak about 'the inescapable God'.

Sunday

O Lord, you have searched me and known me. You know when I sit down and when I rise up; you discern my thoughts from far away (vv. 1–2).

It's easy, Lord, to awaken in the morning and be filled with thoughts of tasks to do and pressures that can weigh heavily upon us.

Help us to be mindful of your continual presence among us. You know us better than we know ourselves. Help us to use this new morning to its full, allowing its light and vibrancy to fill our hearts.

Guide our thoughts, that we may never be far from your will. Allow your Spirit to breathe through the tasks that lie before us this coming week, and give us a sense of peace and rest on this your day.

Monday

If I take the wings of the morning and settle at the farthest limits of the sea, even there your hand shall lead me, and your right hand shall hold me fast (vv. 9–10).

Thank you, Creator God, for the beauty of this morning.

Help us to remember that our morning is some other land's nightfall. Keep us alert to the needs of our world, that we might see your guiding hand in everything, and your reassuring hand where it is needed.

Our world is a precious thing, yet so often we abuse it. We pray that you will give us the wisdom to be good stewards of your creation. Enable us to challenge those who live only for today, that they might encounter your eternal splendour in the renewal of this morning light.

Tuesday

If I say, 'Surely the darkness shall cover me, and the light around me become night', even the darkness is not dark to you; the night is as bright as the day, for darkness is as light to you' (vv. 11–12).

O God of everlasting glory, we pray for those who will pass into your greater presence this day. Grant to them the light and peace of your sustaining love. Bring comfort to their families, friends and communities.

This morning may be bright to some, yet dark and hopeless to others. We acknowledge that even in times of darkness, your light continually shines. Help us to realize that, even in darkness, new things grow and come into being.

In the early light of morning, we praise you, O loving God. May the dawn light inspire us now and always.

Wednesday

For it was you who formed my inward parts; you knit me together in my mother's womb. I praise you, for I am fearfully and wonderfully made (vv. 13–14a).

O Lord of life and love, we pray for all those to be born this morning. Thank you for the expertise and care that will surround their entry into your world. We pray especially for those who will be born in difficult circumstances.

Thank you, Lord, for all new life. Help us to value those who live around us. We ask that we might learn from children who are filled with wonder and amazement at everything.

Sometimes, Lord, we take the wonder of our own creation for granted. Forgive us for the times we neglect ourselves. May this morning be a chance to reflect on our lives and pray for your grace and mercy in everything we do.

Thursday

Wonderful are your works; that
I know very well (v. 14b).

*Do we really know your works,
O Lord? Look with compassion upon
our ignorance.*

*There are times, Lord, when we feel
distant and alone. With your help, we
remember that we are not alone, for
you are always with us.*

*If we look out of the window this
morning, what do we see? We praise
you for the little things, the things that
don't seem important. Help us to see
the extraordinary in the ordinary. Lift
us out of our selfishness, that we may
see more clearly the evidence of your
works all around us.*

Friday

How weighty to me are your
thoughts, O God! How vast is the sum
of them! I try to count them—they are
more than the sand; I awake—I am
still with you (vv. 17–18).

*O God of all ages, from before time, in
time, and beyond time, our lives are
full of thoughts, racing here and there.*

*How profound it is that our thoughts
are but a few grains of sand on the
seashore, yet how precious are they to
you. Give us faith this morning to
harness our thoughts creatively.*

*We thank you that as we awaken
from our rest you are waiting for us.
Help us to listen to you, wherever we
might be.*

*O God of all ages, pour your
blessings on us, that we might return
them to you in our morning tasks.*

Saturday

Search me, O God, and know my
heart; test me and know my thoughts.
See if there is any hurtful way in me,
and lead me in the way everlasting
(vv. 23–24).

*Challenge me, Lord, this morning.
Where I have caused upset, may I be
gracious in repairing it. Gentle Holy
Spirit, move within us, to awaken,
refresh, test, correct, and inspire.*

*May we glimpse your eternity in the
fresh light of this new day. As we reflect
on this week, thank you for all the
opportunities we have had to serve
you, and forgive us for all the times we
have failed you.*

*Your love is new every morning;
how amazing it is, to dwell in your
light.*

Musings of a middle-aged mystic

Veronica Zundel is a journalist, author and contributor to 'New Daylight'. She has also written 'The Time of Our Lives' for BRF. She lives in north London.

Do you wake in the morning full of joy and ready to face whatever challenges and gifts the day may present? No, nor do I. Mornings are so 'not me'. I don't do mornings. Getting up at 8 o'clock is early as far as I am concerned. That's one of the joys of being self-employed and working at home— though it's one of its hazards too, as it is so easy to waste half the day snoozing or playing Patience games on the computer.

Yet I remember with great pleasure the Easter Sunday sunrise services at a Christian conference centre that I used to visit often. We would gather at 5am in the dewy garden, where there was a little outdoor chapel with a rough log altar and a plain wooden cross. The words 'Praise for the sweetness / Of the wet garden' came alive as never before, and after we had sung and prayed we would repair to the dining hall for coffee and Finnish cinnamon pastries, fresh and warm from the oven. It was a wonderful way of celebrating the resurrection, that morning of mornings.

Morning has always been a symbol of new beginnings, of restoration and hope. Even in the midst of overwhelming grief, the author of

Lamentations can declare, 'His mercies... are new every morning' (3:22–23, NRSV). The psalmist announces, 'Awake, my soul! ... I will awake the dawn' (Psalm 57:8), which suggests that he was a better early riser than I am. Isaiah promises Israel that 'your light shall break forth like

> **One unimaginable day, there will be a morning without clouds**

I'm heartened by the fact that, in the creation story, each day begins not with morning, but with evening

the dawn' (58:8) and that 'nations shall come to your light, and kings to the brightness of your dawn' (60:3).

The phrase 'a new dawn' has become a favourite promise of politicians and a common image on posters like those Communist era ones that show a noble worker striding out against a rising sun, with the legend 'Forward to the next Five-Year Plan'. Yet for the guilty or the depressed, morning can mean nowhere to hide, or the start of another day full of difficult tasks and obligations. God, in the book of Job,

describes the dawn as taking hold of the skirts of the earth and shaking the wicked out of it (38:12–13), a vivid picture of the impact new light has on those who (for whatever reason) prefer the darkness. To look forward to each new morning without the dread of repeating yesterday's failure can seem a hope beyond reach for those whose life, whether by their own fault or through circumstances, has become hard to bear.

Can morning really be a joy to someone like myself who has to drag herself out of bed, and who on some days can't wait for sleep? I'm heartened by the fact that, in the creation story, each day begins not with morning, but with evening: 'And there was evening and there was morning, the first day' (Genesis 1:5). Jews still begin the sabbath with the festive family meal of Friday night, not with Saturday morning's service. Perhaps, while God in Genesis rests after the work of creation, people who inhabit the world made by God are allowed to rest *before* doing their work.

Certainly it's true that for some of us, there has to be a lot of darkness and night before there is a glimpse of morning, but I've never known a night that didn't eventually end with the sunrise, even if that sunrise happened behind clouds. And the promise still holds: one unimaginable day, there will be a morning without clouds, internal or external. One day, morning will come and never leave. ∎

Do take a moment to visit the *Quiet Spaces* website (www.quietspaces.org.uk) and email us with your thoughts, perhaps sparked by what you have read in this issue.

In our next issue

Noel Coward declared that 'mad dogs and Englishmen go out in the midday sun'—so is noon the time for rushing around and getting lots done (making the most of the day) or the chance for a siesta, finding a quiet space somewhere in the shade? Our next issue of *Quiet Spaces*, 'Noon', considers the need for 'seizing the moment', making the most of the opportunities God gives us, and also the importance of pausing to rest and reflect.

Contact us at:

Quiet Spaces,
BRF,
15 The Chambers,
Vineyard, Abingdon
OX14 3FE, UK
enquiries@brf.org.uk

QUIET SPACES SUBSCRIPTIONS

Quiet Spaces is published three times a year, in March, July and November. To take out a subscription, please complete this form, indicating the month in which you would like your subscription to begin.

☐ I would like to give a gift subscription (please complete both name and address sections below)

☐ I would like to take out a subscription myself (complete name and address details only once)

This completed coupon should be sent with appropriate payment to BRF. Alternatively, please write to us quoting your name, address, the subscription you would like for either yourself or a friend (with their name and address), the start date and credit card number, expiry date and signature if paying by credit card.

Gift subscription name _____

Gift subscription address _____

_____ Postcode _____

Please send beginning with the next July / November / March issue: *(delete as applicable)*

(please tick box)	UK	SURFACE	AIR MAIL
Quiet Spaces	☐ £16.95	☐ £18.45	☐ £20.85

Please complete the payment details below and send your coupon, with appropriate payment to: BRF, 15 The Chambers, Vineyard, Abingdon OX14 3FE, United Kingdom.

Name _____

Address _____

_____

Postcode _____ Telephone Number _____

Email _____

☐ Please do not email me any information about BRF publications

Method of payment: ☐ Cheque ☐ Mastercard ☐ Visa ☐ Maestro ☐ Postal Order

Card no. ☐☐☐☐ ☐☐☐☐ ☐☐☐☐ ☐☐☐☐ ☐☐☐☐ ☐☐☐☐

Valid from ☐☐☐☐ Expires ☐☐☐☐ Issue no. of Maestro card ☐☐☐

Security Code ☐☐☐

Signature _____ Date ____ / ____ / ____

All orders must be accompanied by the appropriate payment.
Please make cheques payable to BRF

☐ Please do not send me further information about BRF publications

PROMO REF: QSMORNING

BRF is a Registered Charity